Basic Baroque Re

This book will help you begin to play soprano recorder simply and easily, with no previous knowledge of reading notes. The book includes 18 pictures with fingering positions for the soprano recorder, with pitch names and notations. The musical notes included are:

C D E F F# G A Bb B C D E F G

Low B has 2 alternate fingerings. Low F, Low F#, and High F have different fingering for Baroque and German recorders.

These charts are suitable for both popular styles of soprano recorder. The reverse of most pages with fingering chart depict the sheet music for a simple song, with a letter above each note.

You can cut the pages out of the book and use them as flashcards.

Baroque & German Recorders

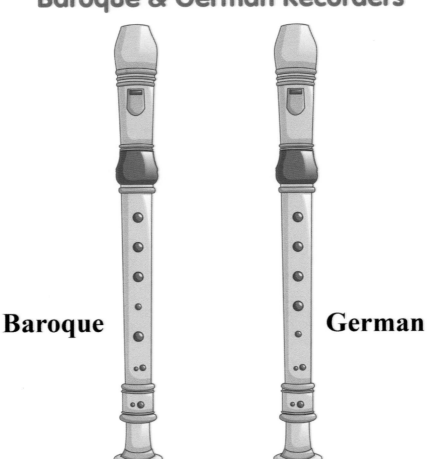

Baroque   **German**

Basic German Recorder Charts

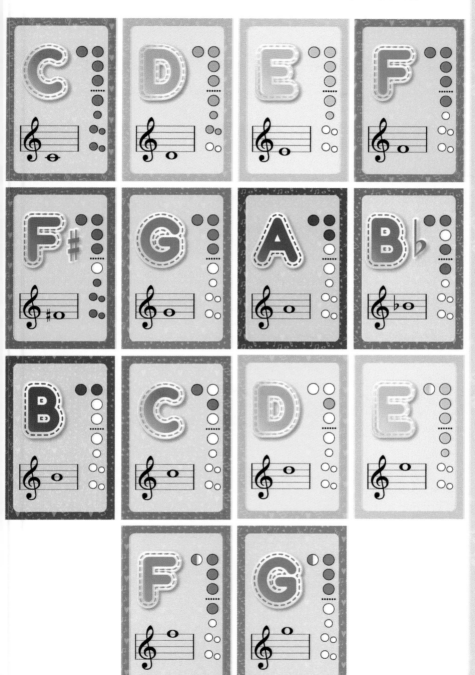

How to hold a recorder

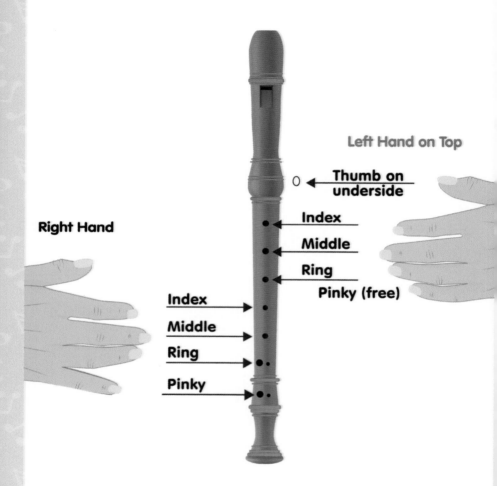

Left Hand on Top

Thumb on underside → O

Index
Middle
Ring
Pinky (free)

Right Hand

Index →
Middle →
Ring →
Pinky →

Recorder Essentials

- Left hand on top
- Left thumb positioned on underside
- Cover the holes completely
- Blow gently and lightly but steadily
- Whisper the syllable "too" or "doo" for each note

Happy Birthday

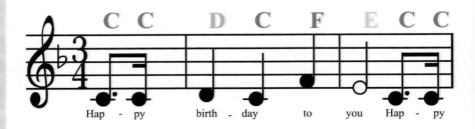

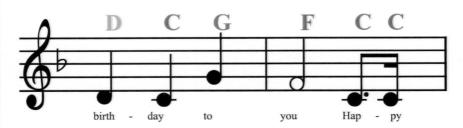

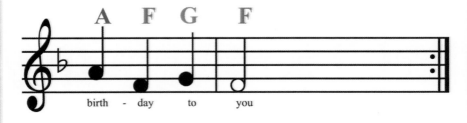

Do You Know the Muffin Man?

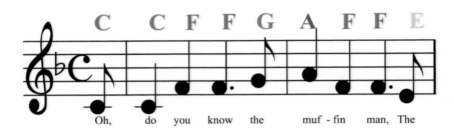

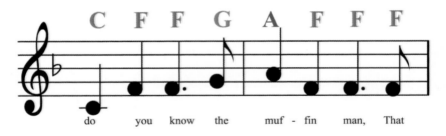

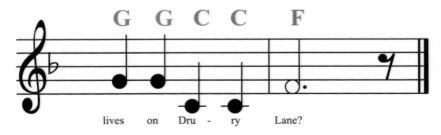

Row, Row, Row Your Boat

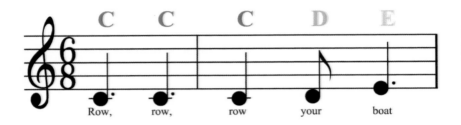

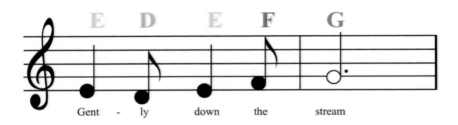

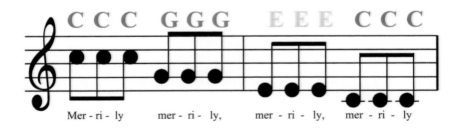

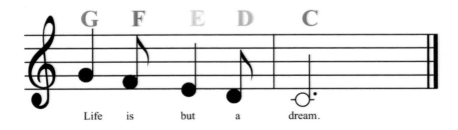

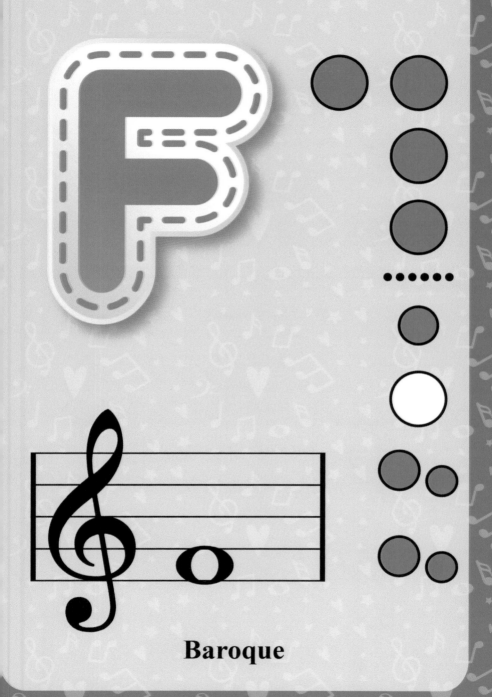

Baroque

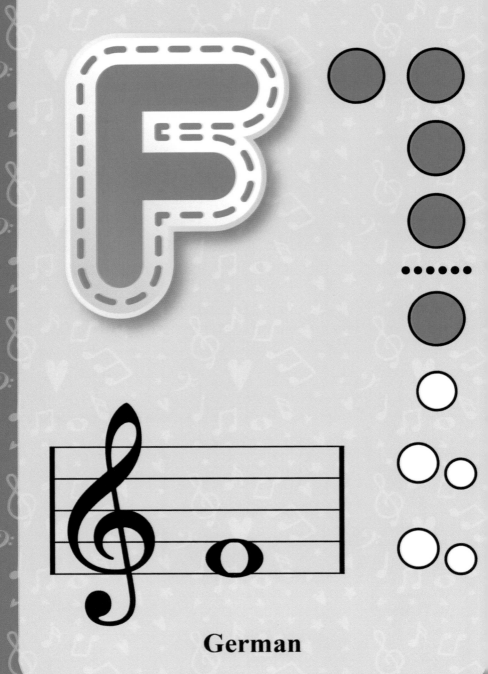

German

Baroque

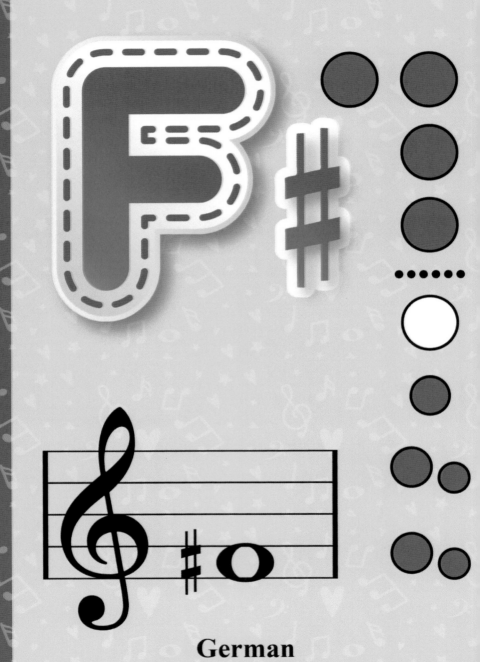

German

Mary Had a Little Lamb

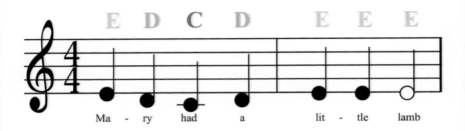

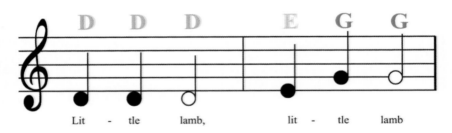

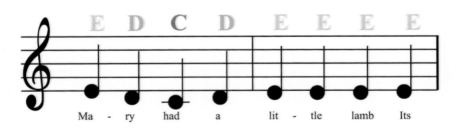

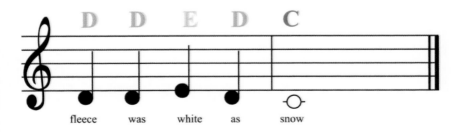

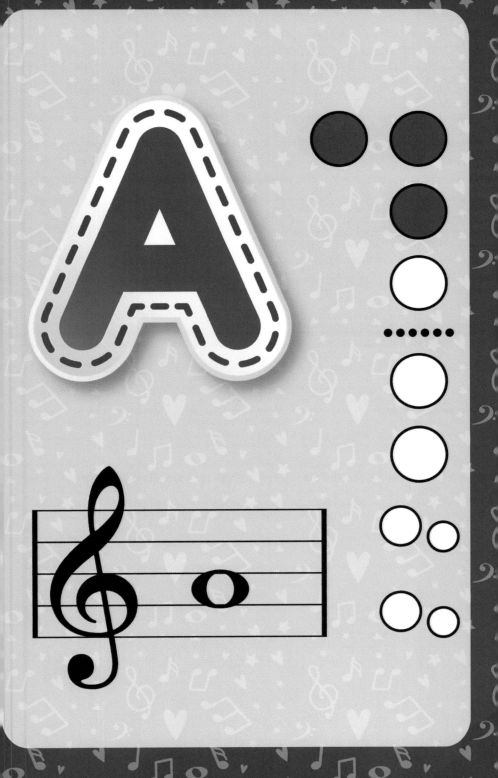

The Wheels on the Bus

The wheels on the bus go round and round,

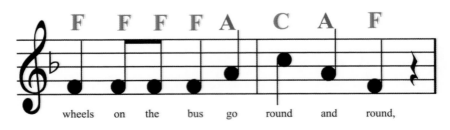

round and round, round and round, the

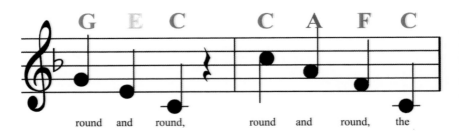

wheels on the bus go round and round,

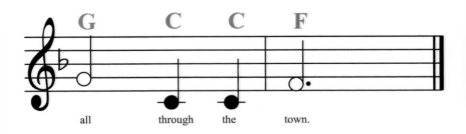

all through the town.

London Bridge is Falling Down

**Alternate
Fingerings**

Five Little Ducks

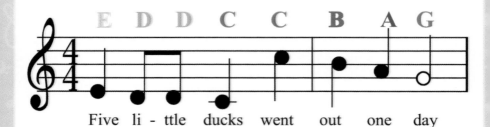

Five li - ttle ducks went out one day,

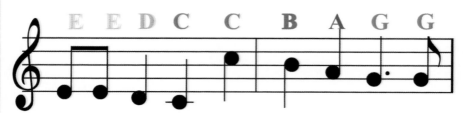

O - ver the hill and far a - way

Mo - ther duck said, "Quack, quack, quack, quack", and

on - ly four li - ttle ducks came back.

Cobbler, Mend My Shoe

Ring Around the Rosie

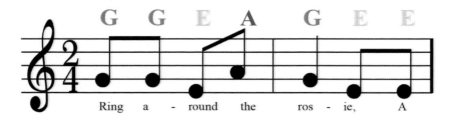

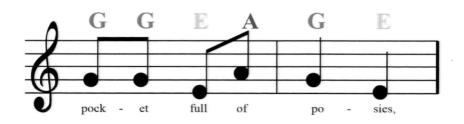

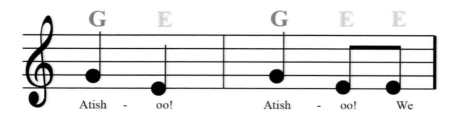

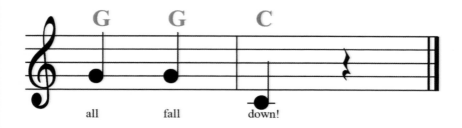

Baroque

German

Rain, Rain, Go Away

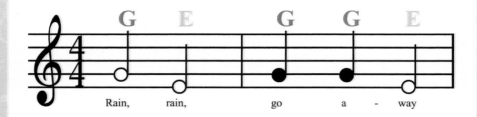

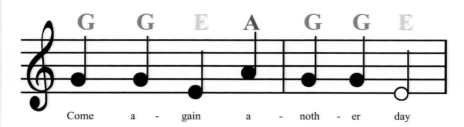

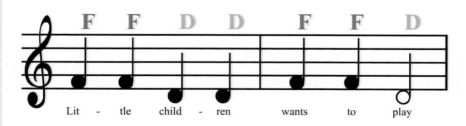

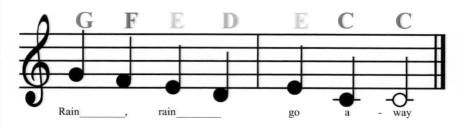

Baby Bumble Bee

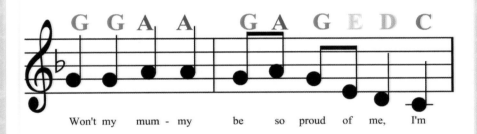

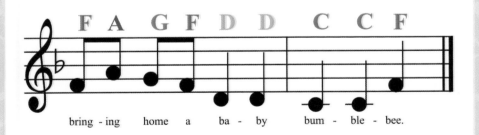

Printed in Great Britain
by Amazon

47461254R00021